For John, whose love and
faithfulness give me courage.
–Kristen

To my husband, Steven,
who always believes in me.
–Debbie

This book belongs to

Can you find 19 hidden cameras in this book?

GOOD PICTURES BAD PICTURES™ jr.

A Simple Plan to Protect Young Minds

By Kristen A. Jenson, MA
Illustrated by Debbie Fox

GLEN COVE PRESS™

We see lots of pictures everywhere.
Where do we see them?

On our walls.

In books and
magazines.

On signs along roads
and on buildings.

On television,
computers
and screens.

Good pictures show beautiful and interesting parts of our world.

We love pictures of
cute baby animals.

We have fun watching good movies and videos.

We enjoy looking at pictures of our family and friends.

These good pictures help us remember the people we love.

What good pictures do you like to look at?

Some pictures
are good.

But some pictures are not good. They're bad for you.

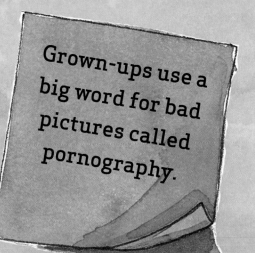

Grown-ups use a big word for bad pictures called pornography.

Bad pictures show
the private parts of
the body that we cover with a swimsuit.

These parts are
meant to be kept private.

15

Every part of your body is good, including your private parts. But taking pictures of them is *not* good.

When people
show pictures
of private parts,
they aren't
private anymore.

It's important to
keep private parts
private!

Where might we see bad pictures?
The same places we can see good pictures!
On screens like a phone or a tablet.

On television or on a computer. In magazines. On signs in stores or on billboards along roads.

No matter where you see bad pictures, they are not safe for kids to look at.

Some things are safe
and some things are *not* safe.
Some things are very dangerous!

Many things are not safe to eat or drink. They are poisonous and can make you very sick!

Good pictures are safe to look at.

Bad pictures are *not* safe to look at.

Bad pictures are like **picture poison** for your brain! Looking at them is dangerous for a growing child.

Sometimes kids see bad pictures by accident.

But even if you see a bad picture, that doesn't make you a bad kid.

Have you ever seen a picture, cartoon or video of people with no clothes on showing their private parts?

If you have, don't worry! There's something *good* you can do if you see a bad picture.

Yes? Where did you see it?

If you ever see a bad picture, video or cartoon of people with no clothes on, here's what to do to stay safe:

 **Turn** **Run**   **Tell**

Turn away from
the bad picture.

Practice this!
Turn your head
and cover your
eyes with
your hands.

Run and find your parents or an adult you trust.

Practice this!
Pretend you're running! Move your arms back and forth.

Tell them what you saw.
Say, "I just saw a bad picture!"
Never keep bad pictures a secret from your parents.

Practice this!
Cup your
hands around
your mouth.

Remember these five safety rules:

1. If someone tries to show you bad pictures or videos, look away. Remember to *Turn, Run, and Tell!*

2. If you ever see a bad picture or video, *never* show it to another child.

3. No one should ever take pictures or videos of you without your clothes on. If someone ever tries to do that, tell your mom or dad or a trusted adult right away!

4. Never take pictures or videos of yourself without clothes on.

5. If you see a bad picture or video and it keeps popping up in your mind, go and tell mom or dad or a trusted adult.* Say, "I need your help to make the bad picture go away."

*Parents, refer to *Notes to Parents and Caregivers* for advice on helping kids learn to "forget" bad pictures.

You have the power!

You can remember to
Turn, Run, and Tell
when you see a bad picture.

You can be happy and
safe if you choose to look
at good pictures!

Grab your free
**Turn, Run,
and Tell** BONUS!

Notes to Parents and Caregivers

HOW TO USE THIS BOOK

Congratulations for being proactive!

As you read *Good Pictures Bad Pictures Jr.* with your child, you'll see **optional messages and discussion questions in the form of "sticky" notes.** Feel free to read them to your child or skip them entirely.

Also included in the sticky notes are suggested **physical actions kids can use to practice the *Turn, Run and Tell* plan.** These will help your kids remember exactly what to do when they see bad pictures. And they're fun!

Another fun feature is the **19 hidden cameras** that your child can find throughout the book. Looking for them can help to keep your child's attention.

WHY YOU'RE DOING THE RIGHT THING

Parents who arm their young children against the dangers of pornography are defending their child's innocence. Kids who are left alone to deal with exposure to pornography themselves are at much greater risk for the following reasons:

- Pornography is routinely used by perpetrators to groom young children for sexual abuse.

- Kids are wired to imitate what they see. Viewing pornography increases the risk of child on child sexual abuse.

- Young children are becoming addicted to pornography with serious, lifelong consequences.

Experts in child sexual abuse prevention and pornography addiction recovery advise parents to begin educating kids about online dangers **as soon as they have any access to the internet.** This includes access from mobile devices owned by friends, family members, teachers, fellow students and babysitters.

To defend the young minds in your care, be your child's first and best source of information about how to recognize and reject pornography.

HOW TO RESPOND

You may have mixed feelings when your child uses the *Turn, Run and Tell* plan to report an exposure to pornography. It's normal to feel upset that your child was exposed and happy that your child did the right thing by coming to tell you.

I encourage you to put a big smile on your face and give your child a hug when this happens! Assure them by saying, "Thank you for telling me. You did the right thing!"

Then, when you are calm, follow up with a few gentle questions:

- "Tell me what happened."

- "What did you see?"

- "How did it make you feel?"

Depending on the type of pornography they see, kids will have a variety of reactions. Some are shocked, others are sickened, and still others are intrigued and want to see more. Some kids are confused because they experience all three reactions at the same time. (If your child has seen something particularly traumatic, you may want to engage professional counseling for additional support.)

The most important part of this is to listen, acknowledge your child's feelings, and don't shame them in any way. You may want to follow up with some phrases like these:

- "I'm sorry you had to see this."
- "Kids shouldn't have to see bad pictures."
- "I'm happy you told me! That was a good decision."

NOTE:

The simplest way to define pornography for a young child is by describing nudity that focuses on the private parts of the body. Not all nudity is pornographic, but anytime your child sees nudity, especially on a screen, they should tell you. For more ideas on "Art vs. Porn" see our articles at DefendYoungMinds.com.

HOW TO HELP A CHILD FORGET BAD PICTURES

Pornography makes very powerful memories in a child's mind!

That is why young kids need their parent's help. "Forgetting"

or neutralizing a pornographic image is simple but takes practice and guidance. Essentially, instead of trying to forget an image or video, a child needs to create a new neural pathway away from the memory of pornography. Here's how:

1. **Help your child identify a special, fun or exciting activity they *love*.** Maybe it's a song, a funny part of a movie, a toy, or a physical activity. It can be anything they enjoy that helps to distract them.

2. **Teach your child to think about that special fun activity whenever a bad picture pops up in their mind.** Doing something physical that requires mental concentration can also help distract a child from focusing on the memory of the bad picture.

3. **Encourage your child to keep practicing.** Their mind will naturally return to the strong memory of pornography. That's OK. Every time that happens, ask them to think of their special fun activity. It will take practice, but as they work at it, the bad memory will pop up less frequently in their mind and have less power over them.

YOU CAN DO THIS!

You can use this book over and over again as you regularly fortify your children against the unhealthy sexual messages so prevalent in our society. Children *can* learn to reject pornography and the harms that come with it. They deserve to be warned and protected early enough to keep themselves safe.

Keep arming your child with *Good Pictures Bad Pictures*!

When your child is 7-8 years old, begin reading the next bestselling book in the series: *Good Pictures Bad Pictures: Porn-Proofing Today's Young Kids*. They'll learn these five powerful digital defense lessons:

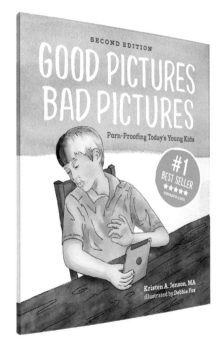

- **How to recognize pornography by the way it makes them feel.** (This is so important in helping kids reject it.);

- How looking at pornography can become a **real addiction**, like drugs or alcohol;

- How to keep **their *thinking brain* in charge** of their *feeling brain* to stay safe;

- How to keep their *attraction center* from being **tricked** by pornography; and

- How to use the **CAN DO Plan** to effectively reject every exposure to pornography.

Good Pictures Bad Pictures uses simple, kid-friendly analogies to help children install an *internal* filter and protect their own brain.

What parents, grandparents, and experts are saying about this groundbreaking tool

"As a psychologist and mother of four, I can't recommend this book highly enough. Pornography is a fast-track to depression, anxiety, and unhealthy relationships between males and females."

"Completely appropriate for young children even if you haven't had the birds and bees talk."

"My clients read *Good Pictures Bad Pictures* to their children to explain how compulsive porn has impacted mom, dad and/or siblings. This book gives clients the opportunity to shine light on compulsive porn use in an age appropriate way."

CASSIE KINGAN, MA, PC, CCPS, CCTP

"*Good Pictures Bad Pictures* is the practical, positive, and powerful tool families need. I whole-heartedly recommend reading this with your children regularly so they will develop self-control—the ultimate protection from pornography."

VAUNA DAVIS, FOUNDER OF REACH1O

"Kristen Jenson has given us a remarkable and timely tool to teach the neuroscience of avoiding pornography addiction in a way kids can easily understand."

DONALD L. HILTON JR. MD, PRACTICING NEUROSURGEON AND CLINICAL ASSOCIATE PROFESSOR, UNIVERSITY OF TEXAS, SAN ANTONIO

Visit DefendYoungMinds.com/books to learn more.

THANK YOU TO ALL THE PEOPLE WHO HELPED WITH THIS BOOK!

Hannah Allen, parent, Vancouver, Washington

Melody Bergman, parent, editor, Midlothian, Virginia

Stephen and Rhyll Croshaw, grandparents, directors of SALifeline Foundation, Lehi, Utah

Debbie Fox, grandparent, illustrator, Provo, Utah

Kate Fricke, parent, Rigby, Idaho

Claudine Gallacher, parent, Santa Barbara, California

Lori Gelwix, grandparent, Richland, Washington

Dawn Hawkins, parent and CEO, National Center on Sexual Exploitation, Washington, D.C.

David and Melissa Hunsaker, parents, Salt Lake City, Utah

Ramona Zabriskie, grandparent, author, speaker, Ridgefield, Washington

Nicole Liebert, parent, Richland, Washington

Robin Jorgensen, parent, Richland, Washington

Emily Kidder, parent, Kennewick, Washington

Evan MacDonald, parent, graphic designer, Monroe, Washington

Natalie Murrow, parent, Dayton, Ohio

Trisa Perry, parent, Richland, Washington

Amber Perry, parent, Richland, Washington

Nicole Petersen, M.Ed, grandparent, Child Protective Services investigator, Bothell, Washington

Stacey Roundy, parent, Bellevue, Washington

Kari Williams, parent, Richland, Washington

CONNECT WITH KRISTEN

Let me know what you think of *Good Pictures Bad Pictures Jr: A Simple Plan to Protect Young Minds*! Find me on Facebook (Kristen A. Jenson Author) and check out my website DefendYoungMinds.com where you can find research-based parenting guides and my constant stream of articles on timely topics.

Follow my work at Defend Young Minds on social media. ⃝ 🐦 f ⓟ

Empowered.
Resilient.
Screen-smart kids.

CREDITS

Written by Kristen A. Jenson
Illustrated by Debbie Fox
Designed by Evan MacDonald

ISBN: 978-0-997-31872-2

Also available at quantity discounts from Glen Cove Press. Email info@glencovepress for more information.

Printed in the USA. 9th Print Run.

DefendYoungMinds.com/books